blueberry forecast

blueberry forecast

Momin Mirza

For my mother, father, and grandparents.

the forecast today is blueberries

haiku number one:
softboil, halfway done
eggs indeed come straight from the
refrigerator

haiku number two:
two eggs on the plate
hunger eats me inside out
eat tomorrow's food

haiku number three:
what does this look like?
egg, egg, and noodle, noodle
something to eat now

haiku number four:
hello eggsies, hey
put some salt on you today
and some vegetables

haiku number five:
ramen, ramen soup
ramen ramen ramen soup
hungry: add an egg

not a haiku number one:
I eat ramen
I eat egg
I eat ramen with an egg

haiku number six:
eating some bread with
the cheeze and cran apple juice
hello eggy time

haiku number seven:
hungry in the night
am i eating healthy food?
tuna, veggies, egg

haiku number eight:
cooking eggs with yolk
burnt the cheeze but its okay
time to eat the food

haiku number nine:
rice and egg and cheeze
does it go with orange juice?
on the tabletop

haiku number ten:
really old eggs, cooked
frozen strawberry smoothie
met neighbor today

haiku number eleven:
versatile nighttime
it can be so happy too
for now, sadness eggs

haiku number twelve:
burnt myself but now
day ends with happiness. with
eggs and memories

haiku number thirteen:
be at peace tonight
temperamental hunger foe
chicken gratitude

haiku number fourteen:
world is much too big
things change much too slow except
friendship and an egg

haiku number fifteen:
it looks like omelette
but it is just three eggsies
yesterday's old beans

haiku number sixteen:
something made of much
other stuff like veggie burg
burrito with egg

haiku number seventeen:
what is classic? what
fills the void? what's delicious?
you know it is egg

haiku number eighteen:
final dinner here
'fore a month of traveling
egg and nutella

haiku number nineteen:
omelette with such a
hidden surprise. can you guess?
whole egg cooked inside

not a haiku number two:
very neat but slightly burntlet
with my mom a birthday omelette

haiku number twenty:
i had too cook some
dinner for myself tonight
mac, cheeze, plantain, EGG

haiku number twenty one:
noonday smoothie time
the obligatory egg
groundhog day breakfast

haiku number twenty two:
wanted to eat egg
but made mac n cheeze instead
more food from less work

haiku number twenty three:
flipped it late today
turns out it was right on time
better looking egg

haiku number twenty four:
omelette with a juice
bread with cream of cheeziness
appetite for egg

haiku number twenty five:
discrimination
is wrong even with burnt toast
time for lots of jam

haiku number twenty six:
bit mangled omelette
still will taste good though I'm sure
back in country. egg

haiku number twenty seven:
quite a bit spicy
i'm grateful, it still tastes great
omelette fell apart

haiku number twenty eight:
omellete stayed intact
vaccination and late night
requires five egg

haiku number twenty nine:
better omelette now
not quite neat but still more so
than before. it's egg

haiku number thirty:
more like an omelette
but still mostly scrambled, it's
what you'd expect: egg

haiku number thirty one:
boom! kablooie! bam!
violent popping, strange food
why explode, dear egg?

haiku number thirty two:
paratha, milk, and
sauce that goes well with the food
and, of course, the egg

haiku number thirty three:
leaving class right now
breakfast lies in front of me
orange juice, cheeze, egg

Momin Mirza is a graduate of Valparaiso University, twice. He enjoys birdwatching, poetry, literature, and juice, and finds inspiration in the life and books of Mamade Kadreebux.